Countdown to Christmas

Devotions for Families

LAURA K. E. ZIMMERMAN

CPH
SAINT LOUIS

May you have the courage to seek Joy,
The wisdom to know Joy,
And the spirit to share Joy.
—Mark Jennings

To the other joys in my life:
Reid
Ali, Megan, and Hannah
Mom and Dad
Darthy and Lissa

All Scripture quotations, unless otherwise indicated, are taken from the HOLY BIBLE, NEW INTERNATIONAL VERSION®. NIV®. Copyright © 1973, 1978, 1984 by International Bible Society. Used by permission of Zondervan Publishing House. All rights reserved.

The verse marked (Ylvisaker) on page 20 is from "Water, Wind, Fire, and Earth" © 1982 by John Ylvisaker. Used by permission.

Copyright © 1997 Concordia Publishing House
3558 S. Jefferson Avenue, St. Louis, MO 63118-3968
Manufactured in the United States of America

1 2 3 4 5 6 7 8 9 10   06 05 04 03 02 01 00 99 98 97

Contents

Dear Parents,

This book is meant to assist your family as you prepare for the birth of Jesus. It is offered to help children and families focus on the true meaning of Christmas. It begins with the first day of Advent and continues through all twelve days of Christmas. Venturing through this book can help you teach your children that preparation for Christmas is important, but so is the celebration following the birth of our Lord. Because the length of the Advent season varies from year to year, you may need to either skip some of the Advent entries or do a couple each day to reach the Christmas Eve devotion on December 24.

This book can be used in a number of ways, depending upon your family and your desires. Share with your children your own feelings, your personal beliefs, or additional selections of God's Word. Encourage your children to ask questions and to seek further understanding. In this way, they will grow in faith. Teach them the importance of truly understanding the Word of God and His presence in our lives today—not just to a people of long ago.

Each day also has an ornament for you to hang on an Advent Tree. (See instructions at the back of the book.) You may make or find your own three-dimensional ornaments to hang on this tree or you may photocopy and cut out the paper ornaments found in the back of this book. There is also a suggestion for making the Advent Tree itself.

It is my sincere prayer that this book, the message of God's eternal and unconditional love, and the faith your family shares with one another will truly enhance your Advent preparation and Christmas celebration.

Many Blessings,

Lori

The Messianic Rose

Show me Your ways, O Lord, teach me
Your paths; guide me in Your truth
and teach me, for You are God my Savior,
and my hope is in You all day long.
—PSALM 25:4

Today begins the season of Advent. During Advent, we prepare our hearts, our homes, and our lives for the birth of Jesus. Before you were born, a lot was done to prepare for your birth. Your mom made many visits to the doctor. The doctor checked to see how well you were growing by measuring your mommy's tummy and by listening to your tiny beating heart. Family and friends hosted special baby showers for you where they brought gifts to help your family care for you. Your mom and dad read lots of books about pregnancy and babies. Maybe they took classes about how babies are born and what they should do to be ready for you. They prepared a bed for you. Your mom ate foods to help you grow strong and healthy, and probably took vitamins so you would have everything you needed to grow as best you could.

Advent is the time for us to do similar things to get ready for Jesus' birth. You can prepare ornaments for your Advent tree. You can even sing songs. All these activities can help you to prepare to celebrate the time when Jesus came to earth—as a tiny baby just like you once were.

The ornament you will hang on your Advent tree today is called the Messianic Rose. It symbolizes the promised Messiah, Jesus. It is also a symbol of Advent. Advent means the coming or arrival of something really big, something very important. As you hang this little ornament, think about how very special, how extremely important it was for Jesus to be born and to live and to die for us, and how much love and preparation God invested in each of us, because He loves us.

Newspapers

Hear the word of the Lord.
—JEREMIAH 29:20

efore the days of radio and television, before the days of telephone and e-mail, there were newspapers. Newspapers gave people information about the world around them. Newspapers were published daily or weekly and if something really important happened before the paper was due out, if a very important event happened that people needed to know about, the newspaper published a "special edition." This special paper would tell people about an important and all too often tragic event like a war, death, or bombing. When the papers hit the streets, the news carriers shouted, "EXTRA! EXTRA! READ ALL ABOUT IT!!" to tell people about this special edition of the paper, to make them aware of the recent news, and to encourage them to read the important information the paper contained.

Before the days of newspapers and books, stories were told. The important stories of families, of faith, of miracles, were told by those who remembered them or by those who had heard them many times. The Bible is a written collection of such stories. The stories in the Bible are stories of people like Adam and Eve, Noah, and Abraham. Stories of the Israelites' walk through the desert, David fighting Goliath, Peter walking on water. They are stories of miracles—Daniel in the lion's den, the feeding of the five thousand, and the raising of Lazarus from the dead. The Bible is full of stories of love, of anger, of sin and forgiveness. The Bible is full of stories of news— Good News—of God, His people, and His love for each of us. The stories in the Bible are special because the Holy Spirit inspired the people who wrote them down—they recorded history so more people could learn of the Good News of Jesus.

Martin Luther believed it was very important that the stories in the Bible be written in a language people could understand. He wanted all people to be able to "read all about" God and Jesus. Because of his belief (and that of countless other people), the stories of the Bible have been written down and translated into hundreds of languages, allowing millions of people to read and learn from the stories of the Old and New Testaments–just as you will do in the coming weeks.

As you hang the newspaper ornament, be reminded of God's Word to us—so that we may learn and hear the stories of His love and devotion to each of us. And remember how important it is to "READ ALL ABOUT IT!"

Creation

In the beginning God created the heavens and the earth.
Now the earth was formless and empty,
darkness was over the surface of the deep, and the Spirit of God
was hovering over the waters. … And God said,
"Let the land produce living creatures according to their kinds:
livestock, creatures that move along the ground, and wild animals,
each according to its kind." And it was so.
God made the wild animals according to their kinds,
the livestock according to their kinds, and all the creatures that move along
the ground according to their kinds.
And God saw that it was good.
—GENESIS 1:1–2, 24–25

*A*lmost every time we go to church, we say a Creed. When we say a Creed, we are saying out loud the things we believe about God, about Jesus, and about the Holy Spirit. The first thing we say in the Apostles' Creed is: "I believe in God the Father Almighty, Maker of heaven and earth." That means we believe God made each of us and all creatures; that He gave us our bodies and souls, eyes and ears, our ability to think and love. He gives us clothing and shoes, meat and drink, home and family, and everything we have. God gives us everything we need to live each day. He defends us, He protects us, and He loves us—even though we don't deserve it. We all have a place and a purpose in His plan. He made each of us and everyone and everything else. Because God created everything for a special purpose, we have a responsibility to protect and respect all of His creation.

As you hang the creation ornament on your tree today, remember the wonderful, beautiful things God has created and know how thankful your family is that He created you to be a part of it!

Snowflake

John answered them all, "I baptize you with water. But one more powerful than I will come, the thongs of whose sandals I am not worthy to untie. He will baptize you with the Holy Spirit and with fire."
—LUKE 3:16

Water—without it, we couldn't live a week. Without water, we couldn't grow fruits or vegetables, flowers or herbs in our gardens. Without water, we couldn't go swimming or sailing, build a snowman or skate on the ice. Without water we couldn't clean our clothes or our bodies. But too much water can be harmful. Too much water can flood our homes, a blizzard can trap people, and ice storms make traveling dangerous. Water is powerful and important.

Water was also important in the lives of people in the Bible. When Moses and his people left Egypt, God parted the waters of the Red Sea to help them escape from Pharaoh's men. When they were living in the wilderness, God made bitter water sweet for the people to drink. When Jesus was beginning His ministry, He turned water into wine. When the disciples in the boat were frightened by a storm, Jesus calmed the waters. After Jesus fed the five thousand, He and Peter walked on water. And Jesus used water to wash the feet of His disciples before the Last Supper.

One of the greatest things we do with water is baptize. When you were baptized, water was used in the name of God the Father, God the Son, and God the Holy Spirit to claim you as God's child forever.

As you hang the snowflake ornament, remember the importance of water, the miracle of your baptism, and God's outpouring of love and forgiveness for each of us.

Balloon

When the day of Pentecost came, they were all together in one place. Suddenly a sound like the blowing of a violent wind came from heaven and filled the whole house where they were sitting. They saw what seemed to be tongues of fire that separated and came to rest on each of them. All of them were filled with the Holy Spirit and began to speak in other tongues, as the Spirit enabled them.
—ACTS 2:1–4

Winds may bring rain, cold, or heat. Winds may cool us with their movement or frighten us with their violence. Gentle winds can move a sailboat, lift a kite, or blow a bubble. Fierce winds can level a house, break a tree, or flip a car. When God formed people from the dust of the earth, He breathed into them the breath of life.

On the day of Pentecost, the birthday of the Church, God sent His Holy Spirit to His people with a sound like rushing wind. It is the Holy Spirit who gives us faith to believe in Jesus and share God's love with others. It is the Holy Spirit who spreads God's Word through the whole world.

Inflate a balloon with the wind from your body and tape it to today's ornament. Hang it on your tree tonight. In the coming weeks, you will probably notice the balloon becoming smaller as the wind escapes. As this happens, think of God's Holy Spirit moving through you and the good works that may be happening to others because of what you do and say. Perhaps God is using you right now to bring joy, love, or peace to someone's life. All the air will eventually escape from your balloon but the Holy Spirit will keep filling you up with God's love and energy to serve other people.

Matches

*The fire must be kept burning on the altar
continuously; it must not go out.*
—LEVITICUS 6:13

Fire—just like water and wind, is good, but too much can destroy. Fire can bring warmth to cold nights and light to dark places. We use fire to cook our food, celebrate our birthdays, and make metals. But fire can also kill and destroy. Fire burns homes, forests, and sometimes people.

In the Old Testament, God spoke to Moses through the fire of a burning bush. He led the Israelites through the desert with a pillar of fire. And the people used fire to offer sacrifices to God.

Fire is used as part of our worship services when we light candles on the altar or when we light a baptismal candle. During Advent, we celebrate with fire when we light even more candles on the Advent wreath. One special fire found in many churches burns in what is called the eternal candle. It is a special fire that always burns and should remind us of God's eternal—or forever—love for each of us. This fire is always with us as a reminder of God's promise that He will always be with us.

As you hang the ornament of matches on your tree, remember the light and warmth of fire and of God's eternal love for each of us.

Stone

The earth is the LORD'S and everything in it, the
world, and all who live in it; for He founded it
upon the seas and established it upon the waters.
—PSALM 24:1–2

"Water, wind, fire and earth! These are the things that gave us birth! I'm a child of God! You're a child of God!" (Ylvisaker)

We have celebrated three of these important elements and today we celebrate the fourth, our earth. Earth is the planet on which we live—third planet from the sun in the galaxy of the Milky Way, just a tiny speck of dust in a huge, huge space. It is the only planet in our galaxy on which we can live. On our earth, we grow our food, build our homes, run and play, laugh and cry. We breathe and grow, live and die. God created this earth for us. Our earth provides us with so many of the things we need to survive—coal, oil, iron ore, oxygen, nitrogen, water, animals, and more.

Today's ornament is a stone which represents our earth. As you hang it, remember the beautiful earth God made for us, where He continues to give us life and help us grow, because He loves us.

Apple

---

*Get rid of all bitterness, rage and anger, brawling and
slander, along with every form of malice. Be kind and
compassionate to one another, forgiving each other,
just as in Christ God forgave you.*
—Ephesians 4:31–32

People sin. We do bad things. We think mean thoughts. We say hurtful
words. It wasn't always that way. When God first created people, He
formed us in His image. Adam, the first man, and Eve, the first woman,
lived perfectly in a beautiful garden called Eden. There were no hurtful or sad things
then. Adam and Eve enjoyed everything in God's creation and could do anything
they wished—almost.

In the middle of the garden stood the tree of the knowledge of good and evil. God told Adam and Eve not to eat the fruit of this tree or they would die. Adam and Eve ate the fruit of the tree and God was angry about their sin. They had to leave His beautiful garden and life became more difficult for them.

Because Adam and Eve disobeyed God, sin and pain and death entered our world. The apple ornament you hang on your tree today reminds us of the fruit from the tree of the knowledge of good and evil, of Adam and Eve's first sin, and of God's forgiveness. It also reminds us that God loves us so much that He sent His Son, Jesus, to die for all our sins. Because Jesus died and rose again, we know that, one day, we will be able to live with Him forever.

Rainbow

---

*And God said, "This is the sign of the covenant I am making
between Me and you and every living creature with you, a
covenant for all generations to come: I have set My rainbow
in the clouds, and it will be the sign of the covenant between
Me and the earth. Whenever I bring clouds over the earth
and the rainbow appears in the clouds, I will see it and
remember the everlasting covenant between God and all
living creatures of every kind on the earth."*
—GENESIS 9:12–16

*H*ave you ever seen a prism bend light? Instead of just shining through, like a window, the light from a prism is bent into the colors red, orange, yellow, green, blue, indigo, and violet—like a rainbow. These colors may bounce on the wall or the floor, making a room look cheery. Have you ever wondered about God's rainbows in the sky? They, too, are a result of light being bent, but they mean much more than that.

Long, long ago, there lived a man who loved God. His name was Noah. Because of God's grace, Noah and his family survived a flood that destroyed the rest of the earth. Because of God's love for all of us and His creation, two of every animal also survived this terrible flood. After the flood, God made a promise to Noah that He would never again destroy the earth. The "bow in the clouds" is a symbol and a reminder of this promise to Noah and to us.

As you hang your rainbow ornament, remember the promise God made to us because He loves us.

Lamb's wool

The next day John saw Jesus coming toward him and said, "Look, the Lamb of God, who takes away the sin of the world!"
—JOHN 1:29

Long ago, people offered sacrifices to God. These sacrifices were burned on an altar. People would sacrifice bulls, or sheep, or doves, or other animals. They did this because God had commanded it. It was a picture for them of the promised Messiah's sacrifice, but some people thought it would help them earn God's forgiveness for wrong things they had done. The priests offered sacrifices to

God on behalf of the people and there were special laws about how to offer a sacrifice. People were very worried about their sinfulness and the things they needed to do to earn God's forgiveness.

Because Jesus died for us and our sins, we don't have to offer sacrifices to God. We don't earn forgiveness, God gives it freely. Sometimes Jesus is called the Lamb of God because He was sacrificed for our sins—can you imagine that? He died for us! He died and rose from the dead and He lives again with God. Because of Jesus, God forgives all the wrong we do—all the bad things, the bad thoughts, even the things we don't do that we should have done!

When you hang the lamb's wool ornament on your tree, remember the sacrifice Jesus made for us so that we would be forgiven forever.

Clown

Rejoice in the Lord always. I will say it again:
Rejoice!
—PHILIPPIANS 4:4

When Abraham was ninety-nine years old, God told him that he and Sarah, his wife, would have a baby. Abraham laughed. Sarah laughed. They were very old. Sarah hadn't had any children and now, they thought, they were too old. They thought God was joking. But they were wrong. Sarah did have a baby and they named him Isaac, which means laughter.

Sometimes it seems that people think God is always serious. They think that, as Christians, we should always be serious and somber. They think we should never laugh or giggle in church, because it is God's house and He just wouldn't like it. They think that laughter isn't very respectful or proper.

Fortunately, that isn't true. One of the best gifts God gave us is laughter. God wants us to be happy. He wants us to find great joy in the world He created. In the Psalms, we are told to "make a joyful noise to the Lord." What could be more joyful than sincere and heartfelt laughter? God wants us all to share the joy of the angels when they announced the birth of Jesus, the joy of the wise men when they found the Baby Jesus, and the joy of Mary when she learned Jesus was raised from the dead. God is not angered by laughter; He is worshiped through joyful noise.

When you hang the clown ornament on your tree, think of all the good and joyful things you have been given and thank God for all of them—rejoicing most of all in Him.

Crown

For to us a child is born, to us a son is given, and the government will be on His shoulders, And He will be called Wonderful Counselor, Mighty God, Everlasting Father, Prince of Peace. Of the increase of His government and peace there will be no end. He will reign on David's throne and over his kingdom, establishing and upholding it with justice and righteousness from that time on and forever. The zeal of the LORD Almighty will accomplish this.
—ISAIAH 9:6–7

A crown is a symbol of power and control. Long ago, in many parts of the world, nations were ruled by kings and queens. The Old Testament is full of stories about kings—wise kings like Solomon, good kings like Josiah, and evil rulers like Jezebel and Manasseh.

The prophets of the Old Testament, like Isaiah, promised the Jewish people a king—a great king—a king even greater than King David. They expected a king with authority, one who would be called "Wonderful Counselor, Mighty God, Everlasting Father, Prince of Peace," to come and rule them. This king would establish justice, righteousness, and endless peace. He would rule the whole earth.

The Jewish people knew kings. They heard these stories about the great king told over and over for generations. They looked for this good and powerful king to come to them. They longed for this wise king whose word was law and whose justice was fair. At the time of Jesus, the Jewish people were ruled by a Roman emperor, Caesar Augustus, and they wanted a king to kick the Romans out and restore Jewish rule. They wanted a king who was better than all other kings. The One they received was the King of Kings and Lord of Lords. They expected an earthly king with a crown of gold and a high throne; they got a heavenly king with a crown of thorns and a cross. They expected a great and conquering king; they got a king who rode a donkey. They looked for a great and powerful leader; they received a tiny, helpless baby. They got all they really wanted, but not at all in the way they expected. They didn't get what they expected, but they received more than they ever dreamed.

As you hang the crown ornament, remember that Jesus is your King—wiser than Solomon, more powerful than David, and kinder than Josiah. God knew what we needed and He sent it for us—before we even knew enough to ask.

Feather

"Because he loves me," says the LORD, "I will rescue him; I will protect him, for he acknowledges My name. He will call upon Me, and I will answer him; I will be with him in trouble, I will deliver him and honor him.
—PSALM 91:14–15

When the time comes for young eagles to learn to fly, the mother takes the eaglet upon her wing and flies high above the earth. She shakes the tiny bird off, forcing it to make its first attempt at flying. If she sees her baby in any trouble, she dives beneath it, catches it in her wings, and flies high again to repeat the process until the baby learns to fly.

Our own parents are like the eagle. They love us and never want to see us hurt. When we try new things and explore new places, they want to protect us so that we never need to be afraid and will never be in pain. Our parents want us to learn from their mistakes so we don't hurt in the same way they once did. Sometimes, though, bad things happen. The eaglet might crash; we might trip on the rug or fall from a tree. Our parents can't protect us from all the bad things in the world.

When really bad and hurtful things happen to us or to those we love, it is important for us to remember that God doesn't cause these things—evil does. God doesn't want us to suffer and hurt but we live in a sinful world and bad things will happen to us and to people we love. Just because we love God, it doesn't mean that we won't ever be sad or hurt again. It doesn't mean that people we love won't die or that all our dreams will come true. The fact that we love God doesn't remove the evil and sinfulness from our world.

Remember, as you hang the feather ornament, that even though bad things happen, God will never leave you. God will always love you. He will always be there to pick each of us up when we fall and to hold us when we hurt. He will help us heal and help us try again. He will always be our God.

Fish

Jesus called His disciples to Him and said, "I have compassion for these people; they have already been with Me three days and have nothing to eat. I do not want to send them away hungry, or they may collapse on the way." His disciples answered, "Where could we get enough bread in this remote place to feed such a crowd?" "How many loaves do you have?" Jesus asked. "Seven," they replied, "and a few small fish." He told the crowd to sit down on the ground. Then He took the seven loaves and the fish, and when He had given thanks, He broke them and gave them to the disciples, and they in turn to the people. They all ate and were satisfied. Afterward the disciples picked up seven basketfuls of broken pieces that were left over. The number of those who ate was four thousand, besides women and children.
—MATTHEW 15:32–38

*T*V is short for television. SOS means help. Red lights at a street corner mean stop. People often send messages in codes—numbers stand for letters, symbols stand for words, lights and shapes have meanings. People send messages in codes for fun and for secrecy—and sometimes it's a matter of life and death. Countries send messages in code during times of war so that enemies don't know what they plan to do. Years ago, homeless people in America put a special symbol on certain houses to show that a kind person lived in the house who would feed the homeless. People who hid black slaves as they tried to escape from the south before the Civil War used symbols like the North Star to show that safety and shelter were offered at a particular house.

The Greeks had a word, ΙΞΟΥΣ, which in their language meant fish. To early Christians, this word was a code which meant Jesus Christ, God's Son, Savior. They put the fish symbol on the outside of Christian homes to tell other Christians not to be afraid—they could come here and be safe. At a time when Romans were killing Christians, this code and its symbol saved people's lives. The fish reminded people of Jesus and of miracles.

The fish was also a common food, easily available to people in Jesus' time—just like God is always available to us today. As you hang the fish ornament on your tree, remember it stands for Jesus Christ, God's Son, our Savior, and never forget that Jesus is available to all of us—always.

Watch

Now we see but a poor reflection as in a mirror; then we shall see face to face. Now I know in part; then I shall know fully, even as I am fully known.
—1 CORINTHIANS 13:12

Why is it so hard to wait for some things to happen? It seems like Christmas will never come. Your birthday or summer vacation seem forever away. It's often hard for us to wait even for small things. Sometimes we're hungry and it's hard to wait until supper time. Sometimes we're cold and it seems to take the car forever to warm up.

It's also hard for us to understand certain things. Sometimes things just don't make sense and even moms and dads can't help answer some questions. We wonder why someone we love has died. We wonder why children go hungry. We wonder why families can't love each other the way God intended. The important thing for us to remember is that God has said there is a time for everything—a time to be born, a time to die; a time to weep, a time to laugh; a time to mourn, a time to dance; a time for war, a time for peace—and that God will make everything beautiful in His time. He doesn't cause the bad things to happen, but He promises to make them beautiful. The things that hurt us now will one day make sense. We will one day have answers to all the things we question. We will learn the things we don't understand.

As you hang the watch ornament, remember that time is God's and everything that happens has a time and a purpose—even when we don't understand it.

Whistle

"No one knows about that day or hour, not even the angels in heaven, nor the Son, but only the Father. Be on guard! Be alert! You do not know when that time will come. It's like a man going away: He leaves his house and puts his servants in charge, each with his assigned task, and tells the one at the door to keep watch. Therefore keep watch because you do not know when the owner of the house will come back—whether in the evening, or at midnight, or when the rooster crows, or at dawn. If he comes suddenly, do not let him find you sleeping. What I say to you, I say to everyone: 'Watch!' "
—Mark 13:32–37

We have said that Advent is a time of waiting and preparing for Jesus' birth. We have already spent several days talking about and reading about God. We have thought and heard a lot about what we do to prepare—we make and wrap gifts for people we love, we bake special treats, we decorate our homes and send cards and letters to people we know. We have celebrations and parties. We have done all these things to prepare for Jesus' birth on Christmas Eve.

We should also prepare for Jesus' return to earth. We don't know when that will be—it may be today, or next week, or in 40 years. It's kind of like a race. The runners are at the starting line and the starter has said, "Get ready, get set," and then stopped. The whistle hasn't blown. God has told us to be ready and set for His return. We're just waiting for the "GO!"

There are lots of stories in the Bible about people who weren't ready for things. God wants us to be sure we're ready—anytime—for His return. As you hang the whistle ornament on your tree tonight, think about what God has done to get you ready—so that you can to go live with Jesus when God says, "GO!"

Pine cone

---

*The grass withers and the flowers fall, but the
word of the Lord stands forever.*
—1 PETER 1:24B–25A

By now, many homes have set up their Christmas trees. Evergreen trees are cut from the forests and their needles and branches are covered with tinsel, lights, and favorite family decorations. Presents are placed under these trees as gifts of love for our family and friends. Stars are placed atop trees to remind us of the Christmas star, or angels are set at the top to remind us of the angels in the heavens announcing Jesus' birth.

Evergreen trees have become a symbol for Christmas and we decorate them in our homes in celebration because they are green all year round. They don't lose their leaves like some trees; they hold their needles throughout the year. This reminds us of God's everlasting love for us. His love is with us all year round—through new growth in the spring, throughout the long, hot days of summer, into the shortening and cooling days of fall, and even during the bitter, cold days of winter. While other things change, while people grow and move away, while countries change leadership, while people are born and die, some things don't change. God's Word is forever. God's love is forever. God's presence in our lives is forever.

As you hang the pine cone ornament today, remember the tree from which it came and the "evergreen" love, promises, and presence of God.

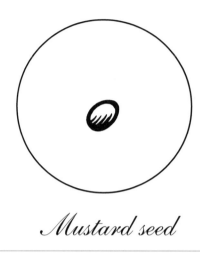

Mustard seed

For God so loved the world that He gave His
one and only Son, that whoever believes in Him
shall not perish but have eternal life.
—JOHN 3:16

F aith is a firm and certain thought or belief. When you plant a seed in the dirt, you believe it will grow. When you walk down the road, you believe the drivers of cars will not try to run you over. When your mom tells you she loves you, you believe her. When your dad asks you to do something and you agree to do it, he believes you will.

Faith in God is belief in His Word, belief in His promises, and belief in His Son. Faith is knowing that our sins are forgiven and that we will one day live forever with God. God even sent His Holy Spirit to fill us with faith in Him because we can't do it on our own. His Holy Spirit keeps our faith strong—even when we feel very alone or afraid.

Life doesn't always make sense. We don't always understand and sometimes we wonder how and why God lets things happen. Sometimes we just have to believe and trust that God will help us make sense of it all someday. Faith in God helps us make sense out of life.

When you hang the mustard seed ornament on your tree, remember the belief a farmer has that the seed will grow. God's Holy Spirit will help your faith to grow as well.

Anchor

And we know that in all things God works for the good of those who love Him, who have been called according to His purpose. ... For I am convinced that neither death nor life, neither angels nor demons, neither the present nor the future, nor any powers, neither height nor depth, nor anything else in all creation, will be able to separate us from the love of God that is in Christ Jesus our Lord.
—ROMANS 8:28, 38–39

An anchor is a symbol for hope. Hope is what helps us believe in the promises of God, even when they seem a long way off. A hope is not like a wish because a wish is often just a dream or fantasy—nice, but not based on anything real. Hope, for Christians, is based on Jesus—His life, His death and resurrection, His love.

Hope is what allows us to celebrate at a funeral for someone we love—that person is with Jesus. Hope that we will see him or her again is what helps keep us going when we are lonely. Hope in Christ is what keeps us going through our problems.

As you hang the anchor ornament today, remember that hope is our anchor when we are happy or sad or tossed about. Hope keeps us from sinking. Hope keeps us from floating away from God. Hope is God's gift until we are with Him in heaven.

Heart

Dear friends, let us love one another, for love comes from God. Everyone who loves has been born of God and knows God. Whoever does not love does not know God, because God is love.
—1 JOHN 4:7–8

"I love you." Moms and dads say it to us, we say it to others. We sing about love, we read about love, we even celebrate love on Valentine's Day. We send cards and candy and we ask those we love to be our Valentine. Sometimes we even say we love things—like pizza, a certain book, or swimming. We fall in love, we fall out of love. Love makes the world go 'round. All's fair in love and war. Love conquers all. Because of the way we overuse the word love, it's sometimes hard to know what a person means when he or she says "love." Does he like you, or does he love you with an everlasting love? Does she like us today, only to dislike us tomorrow? What does she really mean? The love we read about in John is different from all the other love we've talked about. The love John talks about is God's love.

God is love. If you were to draw a picture of God, you would have to draw a picture that shows nothing but love—love that fills heaven and earth. God's love makes us, though we are sinners, lovely. We can love others because God loved us first. Before we were even created, He loved us. He loves us because of who we are—He loves us despite who we are. He loved us so much that He sent Jesus to die for us. He loves us that much!

When you hang the heart ornament on your tree, remember that though we have been blessed with families who love us more than anything else, no one loves us like God loves us, because God is love.

Fishing lure

One day as Jesus was standing by the Lake of Gennesaret, with the people crowding around Him and listening to the word of God, He saw at the water's edge two boats, left there by the fishermen, who were washing their nets. He got into one of the boats, the one belonging to Simon, and asked him to put out a little from shore. Then He sat down and taught the people from the boat. When He had finished speaking, He said to Simon, "Put out into deep water, and let down the nets for a catch." Simon answered, "Master, we've worked hard all night and haven't caught anything. But because You say so, I will let down the nets." When they had done so, they caught such a large number that their nets began to break. So they signaled their partners in the other boat to come and help them, and they came and filled both the boats so full that they began to sink. When Simon Peter saw this, he fell at Jesus' knees and said, "Go away from me, Lord, I am a sinful man!" For he and all his companions were astonished at the catch of fish they had taken, and so were James and John, the sons of Zebedee, Simon's partners. Then Jesus said to Simon, "Don't be afraid; from now on you will catch men." So they pulled their boats up on shore, left everything and followed Him.

—LUKE 5:1–11

*P*eople who make fishing tackle promise that their lures will catch the biggest fish. Television infomercials spend half an hour trying to convince people to buy their product to "catch the big one." People will say this lure is the best, that bait is the best, this hook will work, that line will work. Whole stores sell only fishing equipment and supplies. Strings of cars travel on the freeway at the opening of fishing season. Cars full of people towing boats and all their supplies come hoping to catch fish—lots of fish, big fish, any fish!

Some of the disciples were fishermen. Unlike many people who fish today, Peter, Andrew, James, and John made their living catching fish. They sold them, they ate them—if they didn't catch fish, they didn't have anything. One night, they had been fishing all night and had caught nothing. They must have been very tired, hungry, and disappointed. Jesus came to them. He told them what to do to catch some fish but it didn't make sense. It was the wrong time, the wrong place, and the wrong way, but they caught more fish than their nets could hold.

Miracles happen. They happen at what seems to us the wrong time or the wrong place. The shepherds probably wouldn't have planned the birth of the King in a stable in Bethlehem, but that was the right time and place for the miracle of Jesus' birth. Miracles happen in the way we said they never could—that's what makes them miracles. That's what makes them God's gifts. What seems totally wrong and completely impossible to us is totally right and possible to God. As you hang the lure ornament, remember God's gift of miracles and the wonderful Christmas miracle of love—Jesus our Lord.

Palm

As they approached Jerusalem and came to Bethphage on the Mount of Olives, Jesus sent two disciples, saying to them, "Go to the village ahead of you, and at once you will find a donkey tied there, with her colt by her. Untie them and bring them to Me. If anyone says anything to you, tell him that the Lord needs them, and he will send them right away." ...The disciples went and did as Jesus had instructed them. They brought the donkey and the colt, placed their cloaks on them, and Jesus sat on them. A very large crowd spread their cloaks on the road, while others cut branches from the trees and spread them on the road. The crowds that went ahead of Him and those that followed shouted, "Hosanna to the Son of David!" "Blessed is He who comes in the name of the Lord!" "Hosanna in the highest!" When Jesus entered Jerusalem, the whole city was stirred and asked, "Who is this?" The crowds answered, "This is Jesus, the prophet from Nazareth in Galilee."
—MATTHEW 21:1–3, 6–11

When people traveled by foot and donkey over dirt roads in the Holy Land, a lot of dust was raised. Often, people would spread their robes and palm branches on the ground when important people entered a city. This kept the dust down and was a sign of respect and welcome for kings and generals.

Palm Sunday, when Jesus rode into Jerusalem, thousands of people welcomed Him as a king with palms and lay their cloaks on the ground before Him. They called Jesus the "Bread King." He fed thousands with a few loaves of bread. He performed miracles, He walked on water, He healed the sick, He brought people who were dead back to life. Thousands of people wanted to be near Him—to touch Him. He even had to go out into the sea to sleep on a boat—just to have quiet. These people wanted to make Jesus their king. When He came into the royal city, they expected Him to take over like an army general, and be their king. He could easily have done just that—that's why the Roman guard made plans to kill Him.

The people didn't know that they were indeed welcoming a King—just not the kind they thought. Jesus wouldn't live in an earthly castle and rule from an earthly throne, fighting battles and kicking the Romans out of town. Only a few days after His arrival in Jerusalem, Jesus would be betrayed. He would be accused. He would die on a cross. Hardly what we would expect for a King! This wasn't the end, though. Jesus was also a king who would rise again and live with God forever.

Remember as you hang the palm ornament that Jesus was indeed a king—Jesus is still a king—King of our hearts, King of our lives!

Wafer and grapes

While they were eating, Jesus took bread, gave thanks and broke it, and gave it to His disciples, saying, "Drink from it, all of you. This is my blood of the covenant, which is poured out for many for the forgiveness of sins. I tell you, I will not drink of this fruit of the vine from now on until that day when I drink it anew with you in My Father's kingdom."
—MATTHEW 26:26–29

The night before Jesus died, He celebrated a special dinner with His friends. This dinner was called Passover and it was a special Jewish holiday celebrating the love God showed in protecting His chosen people. During this particular Passover dinner, Jesus did an unusual thing. He took a piece of bread, blessed it, broke it, and gave it to His disciples. He told them to eat the bread and to remember His body—which would hang on a cross for them. A little while later, He took a cup of wine, thanked God for it, and asked for God's blessing. He told His disciples to drink from the cup and remember the covenant which He made with them. He told the disciples that they should remember what He had said and done every time they ate bread and drank wine like this.

The best part of this event was that Jesus died for all people—not just the disciples. His death was for everyone—we are all His chosen people. Each time we celebrate communion, we celebrate the love Jesus has for us. Even if you don't share the bread and wine at God's table yet, it's important for you to know that you are welcome at God's table and you have a very special place there. Very soon, as you learn about God and grow in understanding, you will celebrate fully our Lord's Supper. And one day we will celebrate with all of God's saints in heaven the love Jesus has for us.

As you hang the symbol of the bread and wine on your tree tonight, remember Jesus' body and blood given and shed for all people for the forgiveness of sin.

Ashes

"*By the sweat of your brow you will eat your food until you return to the ground, since from it you were taken; for dust you are and to dust you will return.*"
—GENESIS 3:19

Ashes are a symbol to us that we are a part of the earth. God made us from the dust of the earth. He breathed into our nostrils the breath of life, and we became living beings. We were created from this dust and we will return to this dust. As ashes are the remains of wood and fire, dust is the remains of rocks, mountains, and our bodies.

Ashes are also a symbol of great sadness. Ashes remind us of our death. At one time, it was very common for people to put ashes on their faces to show how sad they were when someone they loved died. Some cultures continue to do this.

We know that death will come eventually. At different times, in different places, and in different ways, we will all die. Because of this, God sent His Son. God sent Jesus to die, and to defeat death by rising again. Because Jesus didn't stay dead, neither will we.

As you hang the ornament of ashes on your tree tonight, remember that ashes can be a reminder of sadness. But for us, as Christians, ashes are a symbol of hope—our reminder that there is something wonderful for us after the death of our bodies—life forever with Jesus!

Ring

Love is patient, love is kind. It does not envy, it does not boast, it is not proud. It is not rude, it is not self-seeking, it is not easily angered, it keeps no record of wrongs. Love does not delight in evil but rejoices with the truth. It always protects, always trusts, always hopes, always perseveres. ...And now these three remain: faith, hope and love. But the greatest of these is love.
—1 CORINTHIANS 13:4–7, 13

When two people fall in love, they sometimes decide to get married. This is a big and serious decision. They, along with their families and friends, will make plans to celebrate their wedding day. They may wear special clothes, they may sing special songs. The church will be decorated and everyone will gather together. The couple will make special promises to each other before their family, their friends, and God. They will also exchange rings. As they do this, the pastor will tell what these rings represent. The rings symbolize love—a love that is pure, true, and precious.

Rings are circles. They are circles that have no beginning and no end—just like God's love for us. He knew us and loved us even before we were born and He will always love us. He loves us when we work and when we play, when we laugh and when we cry.

Rings are also circles that are not broken—just like God's love. God will never stop loving us. The love a husband and wife share is a love that we hope will never end, but for some families it does. That's because we are sinful people and sometimes we fail—even in love—even when we have the best intentions. God's love, however, will never fail. He will never go away from us or get tired of us. He doesn't take vacations or holidays.

When you hang the ring ornament on your tree, remember that no matter what, no matter where, God always loves us with a perfect, eternal love.

Penny

Jesus sat down opposite the place where the offerings were put and watched the crowd putting the money into the temple treasury. Many rich people threw in large amounts. But a poor widow came and put in two very small copper coins, worth only a fraction of a penny. Calling His disciples to Him, Jesus said, "I tell you the truth, this poor widow has put more into the treasury than all the others. They all gave out of their wealth; but she, out of her poverty, put in everything—all she had to live on."

—MARK 12:41–44

*M*oney is mentioned frequently in the Bible. One of Jesus' disciples was a tax collector who took money from the people to give to the government. Many tax collectors were dishonest and taxed people enormous amounts of money—more than they could afford—giving some to the government and keeping some for themselves. Certain people, called slaves, were bought and sold for money, separating families and destroying lives. Jesus warned that too much money could be difficult for people, because they would want to keep it all to themselves and not share it with people who had nothing. Judas received money for identifying Jesus to the people who wanted to kill him. People can use money to do many evil things.

People can also use money to do good things and to help others. The widow in the Bible story had very little money, but she gave it for those who had even less. Money can be used to buy clothing to keep us warm and food for our hungry bodies. Money can be spent to build homes, hospitals, and churches. Many good, important, and necessary things can be done with money.

Money, by itself, is not good or bad. It's what people do—or don't do—with their money that is good or bad. Money can be hoarded and bring no good to anyone. Money can be wasted, spent foolishly, or spent to do things that are hurtful to others. Money can also be shared to help ourselves and other people do good and necessary things. We need to be sure we spend our money to do things that are good and helpful to God and others. We need to give of our money, our talent, our time, and our energy to show God's love for us and for others.

As you hang the penny ornament on your tree tonight, remember the evil and hurtful things people can do with money and think instead of ways to use your money for God's service.

Chi Rho

So for a whole year Barnabas and Saul met with the church and taught great numbers of people. The disciples were called Christians first at Antioch.
—ACTS 11:26

When you were born, you were given a name. Your parents probably chose the name for you. It was not a decision they made quickly, because you would carry the name with you throughout your life. Perhaps you were named after someone your parents loved or respected—what an honor. Perhaps it was just a name they liked—what a joy. Traditionally, when a child is born, he or she is also given the surname, or last name, of the father. You are given this name because you are part of this family—part of the chain of people who can be traced back to certain parents.

When you were baptized, you were also given a name—Christian. It too is a name you will carry forever. You were named after Jesus—what an awesome blessing. He shares His name with you because He loves you and you will always be identified as part of this family of people who believe in Jesus Christ. In this family, you will grow in faith, love, and obedience to the will of God. In this family, you will be welcomed, loved, and cared for. Being part of the family also means you will receive the gifts—or inheritance—that family offers. The inheritance Jesus offers is eternal life with God. You didn't do anything to earn the right to be part of the family. It was God's free gift.

As you hang the Christian symbol tonight, remember the names you have been given and the love with which they came.

Angel

An angel of the Lord appeared to them, and the glory of the Lord shone around them, and they were terrified. But the angel said to them, "Do not be afraid. I bring you good news of great joy that will be for all the people. Today in the town of David a Savior has been born to you; He is Christ the Lord."
—LUKE 2:9–11

An angel is a messenger of God. When angels appear in the Bible, awesome things are about to happen. It was an angel named Gabriel who told Mary that Jesus would grow inside her. It was an angel who told Joseph that Mary should be his wife. It was an angel who appeared to the women at the tomb to tell them that Jesus had risen. The events surrounding the arrival of these angels were no different. It seemed to be an ordinary evening, a night like any other. Shepherds were out with their flocks. It was dark and cold, and they were alone. They couldn't just go to sleep, though—they had to guard their flocks from animals who would kill them, people who would steal them, or natural dangers that may await them. The shepherds had to be alert all the time. They had to be on their guard and ready to respond to any and every danger.

When the angel appeared, the first words he said were, "Do not be afraid." The angel wanted the shepherds to know they did not need to fear because the angel was bringing news of the birth of a baby, news of the birth of a King. The angel brought "Good news of great joy that will be for all the people." The shepherds were among the first to know, because they were alert, they were waiting, they were ready for anything. They had to be—it was part of the job.

When you hang the Christmas angel ornament, remember the fantastic news that the angels brought to the shepherds long ago. Remember to be alert and ready, so you can hear clearly the announcement: this baby—Jesus—was born tonight just for us!

Baby Jesus

In those days Caesar Augustus issued a decree that a census should be taken of the entire Roman world. (This was the first census that took place while Quirinius was governor of Syria.) And everyone went to his own town to register. So Joseph also went up from the town of Nazareth in Galilee to Judea, to Bethlehem the town of David, because he belonged to the house and line of David. He went there to register with Mary, who was pledged to be married to him and was expecting a child. While they were there, the time came for the baby to be born, and she gave birth to her firstborn, a son. She wrapped Him in cloths and placed Him in a manger, because there was no room for them in the inn.
—LUKE 2:1–7

*Y*ou are one of the greatest gifts your parents ever received. Whether you were born into your family or adopted by your family, you were a precious and most beautiful gift of life. Jesus is the greatest gift we all were ever given—another gift of life.

Before Jesus was born, His parents were required to go to Bethlehem. Even though it was very difficult for Mary, she went to be counted with Joseph. While they were away from home, it was time for Jesus to be born. Jesus wasn't born in a modern hospital with doctors and nurses and special equipment like you probably were. Jesus wasn't even born in a home, where He was comfortable and secure. Jesus was born in a stable—a dirty, lonely place with only His mother and father to welcome Him. But God was there, too. God sent Jesus as a tiny baby—just like you once were. God sent Jesus to a family much like yours. God sent Jesus to grow and laugh and play like you do. God sent Jesus to live with us and to show us how we should live. One day, Jesus would even die for us so that we could all live together with Him forever in heaven.

As you hang the symbol of the baby Jesus, remember that Jesus Himself is God's greatest gift to all of us—moms and dads, grandmas and grandpas, kids and adults. Jesus is better than any gift we will open today and more precious than any other we will ever receive. Thank God!

Star

After Jesus was born in Bethlehem in Judea, during the time of King Herod, Magi from the east came to Jerusalem and asked, "Where is the One who has been born king of the Jews? We saw His star in the east and have come to worship Him." When King Herod heard this he was disturbed, and all Jerusalem with him. When he had called together all the people's chief priests and teachers of the law, he asked them where the Christ was to be born. "In Bethlehem in Judea," they replied, "for this is what the prophet has written: "'But you Bethlehem, in the land of Judah, are by no means least among the rulers of Judah; for out of you will come a ruler who will be the shepherd of my people Israel.'" Then Herod called the Magi secretly and found out from them the exact time the star had appeared. He sent them to Bethlehem and said, "Go and make a careful search for the child. As soon as you find Him, report to me, so that I too may go and worship Him."

—MATTHEW 2:1–8

*S*ailors used stars to guide their ships as they crossed the ocean. Explorers used stars to guide them as they mapped new territories. People today still use stars to tell direction, time, and season. Stars guide, and they also announce. Stars tell us of an incredible world—one we can only imagine. Our own sun—so enormous and bright to us—is really just a very tiny star compared with others in our huge universe.

In the vastness of space, thousands of years ago, there was a very special convergence, or coming together, of stars. It was so rare, so different, that it announced to astronomers—and some wise men in particular—that something very special, something incredible, something out of this world was happening. It was the birth of a baby, the arrival of a king—Jesus. Something incredible was indeed happening and the biggest things in the universe—stars—which appear tiny to us, announced the birth of a tiny baby, the biggest event the earth had ever known.

As you hang the star ornament on your tree, remember that Jesus is the star that will guide us, the light that will lead us. We use His example to determine the way we must go.

Birthday candle

---

*When Jesus spoke again to the people, He said,
"I am the light of the world. Whoever follows
Me will never walk in darkness, but will have
the light of life."*
—JOHN 8:12

D uring the cold Midwestern winters, many cars carry winter survival kits. In case a person has trouble with his or her car, this kit is meant to help until someone can arrive to start the car, pull it out of a ditch, or take the stranded motorist home. Perhaps you have one of these kits in your car. Usually, they have some chocolate bars to eat, a can in which to melt snow to drink, salt to melt icy patches on the road, and other things you might need while stranded in a car waiting for help to arrive.

Perhaps the most important items in this kit are a candle and matches. One single candle, in the darkness, can give an incredible amount of light and warmth. This light can help us find our way in the darkness of our world. This warmth can help keep us alive in the coldness of winter. The light and warmth give us hope and comfort while we are waiting for help to arrive. Jesus said, "I am the Light of the World." The light Jesus gives will never go out. The wind can never extinguish it. Water will never douse it. The wick will never burn away. The light of Jesus will always guide us and forever warm us.

As you hang the candle ornament on your tree, remember the love God has for our world—that He sent His Son to guide and warm, to give us direction and to keep us alive.

Candy cane

"I am the good shepherd. The good shepherd lays down His life for the sheep. The hired hand is not the shepherd who owns the sheep so when he sees the wolf coming, he abandons the sheep and runs away. Then the wolf attacks the flock and scatters it. The man runs away because he is a hired hand and cares nothing for the sheep. I am the good shepherd; I know My sheep and My sheep know Me—just as the Father knows Me and I know the Father—and I lay down My life for the sheep. I have other sheep that are not of this sheep pen. I must bring them also. They too will listen to My voice, and there shall be one flock and one shepherd. The reason My Father loves Me is that I lay down My life—only to take it up again. No one takes it from Me, but I lay it down of My own accord. I have authority to lay it down and authority to take it up again. This command I received from My Father."

—JOHN 10:11–18

*I*n the gospels Jesus told many parables. One of His stories was about a shepherd. It is a shepherd's responsibility to protect his flock of sheep. He leads his sheep to fresh food and good water. His sheep recognize his voice and follow him because they trust him. A shepherd knows each of his sheep. Just as your mom and dad know you from a crowd of hundreds, a shepherd knows each of his sheep. Just as your mom and dad would search forever if you were lost, a shepherd will search for a missing sheep until it is found and returned to the flock. Shepherds and sheep belong together—like a family.

Jesus said, "I am the Good Shepherd." He promised to never leave us. He knows us even better than we know ourselves. He gave His life to save ours. He speaks to us and we hear His voice through the words He spoke that are written in the Bible. If we become lost and wander away from Him, He will search for us and lead us home with the rest of His flock.

As you hang the candy cane ornament (that looks like a shepherd's staff), remember the love a shepherd has for his sheep and the love Jesus has for us—so much that He died for us. Even if we would be tempted to stray away, Jesus will always keep us close to Him.

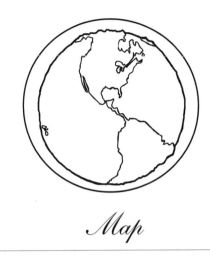

Map

But now, this is what the LORD says—He who created you, O Jacob, He who formed you, O Israel: "Fear not, for I have redeemed you; I have summoned you by name; you are Mine. When you pass through the waters, I will be with you; and when you pass through the rivers, they will not sweep over you. When you walk through the fire, you will not be burned; the flames will not set you ablaze. For I am the LORD, your God, the Holy One of Israel, your Savior; I give Egypt for your ransom, Cush and Seba in your stead. Since you are precious and honored in My sight, and because I love you, I will give men in exchange for you, and people in exchange for your life."
—ISAIAH 43:1–4

*B*efore you plan a trip to a new place, you might look at a map. On the map, you look at where you are and where you want to go. On the map, you discover which roads lead to where you wish to go and which roads lead away from your destination. You might discover places to stop along the way—towns of interest, beautiful landmarks, relatives to visit. With careful planning, you will usually complete your trip safely and on time.

Jesus said, "I am the Way." Jesus leads us to God. Heaven is our destination, the place we will go some day. Along the way, we are baptized, we learn and grow and love, we may marry, we may have children. God has special plans in store for us. Good things will happen along our journey, and we will also probably endure some very sad and difficult times. God was there in the beginning, He is with us through our journey, and He will be with us at our death—to see us safely Home.

As you hang the map ornament on your tree, give thanks that Jesus guides us. We will never be hopelessly lost or left alone because He is with us every step of our journey. Through the hills and valleys, Jesus calls us by name. Through the fire and flood, Jesus walks with us. He has redeemed us, He has called us, we are precious to Him and loved by Him—no matter where we are on our journey.

I am the Truth

The truth

"Do not let your hearts be troubled. Trust in God; trust also in Me. In My Father's house are many rooms; if it were not so, I would have told you. I am going there to prepare a place for you. And if I go and prepare a place for you, I will come back and take you to be with me that you also may be where I am. You know the way to the place where I am going." Thomas said to Him, "Lord, we don't know where You are going, so how can we know the way?" Jesus answered, "I am the way and the truth and the life. No one comes to the Father except through Me. If you really knew Me, you would know My Father as well. From now on, You do know Him and have seen Him."

—JOHN 14:1–7

There is a familiar story about a boy who cried "wolf." He was watching his sheep and wanted to see if the townspeople would come to help him, so he yelled, "Wolf!" as loudly as he could. The townspeople, wanting to keep the sheep safe, came running. When they got to the place where the boy and his sheep were, they found the sheep eating peacefully and the boy laughing. It was a joke. The boy did the same thing three nights in a row. Each time the kind-hearted townspeople ran to his aid. Each time, they found the boy laughing at his own cruel joke. On the fourth night, as the boy was watching his sheep, a real wolf attacked the flock. The boy panicked. He needed to get help to chase the wolf away—the wolf was killing his sheep! He cried, "Wolf! Wolf! Wolf!" But this time when the townspeople heard him, they said to each other, "That boy is lying again. There is no wolf. He just wants to make us look foolish. There is no need to run to his aid." And they stayed right where they were. The wolf stole many of the boy's sheep and scattered the rest. The boy finally realized how cruel and wrong his lying had been.

Unlike the boy who cried "Wolf!" Jesus knows how important truth is in a relationship. You can't trust someone who always lies to you, and Jesus wants us to trust Him. You can't believe someone who says things that never come true or never really happen. Jesus said, "I am the truth." Everything Jesus tells us is true—we can count on it. He's not teasing or exaggerating or lying to us—ever. When He said, "The Son of Man is going to be betrayed ..." (Matthew 17:22) He was not lying. When He said, "The Son of Man must suffer many things ... and be killed ..." (Mark 8:31) He was not lying. When Jesus said, "The Christ will suffer and rise from the dead on the third day" (Luke 24:46) He was not lying.

As you hang today's ornament, remember that Jesus doesn't lie—He is truth. All the things He said are true, all the things He said and did can be believed. Rejoice in the promises He has made to us—that He will be with us always, that He is preparing a place for us to live with Him, and that He will return again to bring us home.

Seeds

"You know the way to the place where I am going." Thomas said to Him, "Lord, we do not know where you are going, so how can we know the way?" Jesus answered, "I am the way and the truth and the life. No one comes to the Father except through Me. If you really knew Me, you would know My Father as well. From now on, you do know Him and have seen Him."
—JOHN 14:4–7

We plant a seed. We put this small sphere into the darkness of the earth and we cover it. We sprinkle water upon the seed. The earth provides nutrients and warmth to the seed. Within a matter of days, the seed will miraculously sprout and grow. The seed will bear its fruit, the seed will die, and the cycle will repeat itself. Although the seed looked like nothing special, within itself it contained what it needed to survive—in the proper growing conditions.

Jesus said, "I am the Life." Jesus knew us before we were even born. Before our moms and dads even held us, before our families ever welcomed us home, Jesus knew us. He watched the forming of our hands, He knew the moment of our heart's first beat. He saw the growth of our tiny feet, He witnessed the moment of our birth. He is sometimes called the Author of Life, because He is so involved in the creation of life—human life, plant life, all life.

Jesus not only creates life, He blesses our living. He provides us with food, shelter, friends, family, work, play, all that is good in "life." With Jesus, there is even more than birth and living—there is life after the death of our bodies. Without Jesus, death and hell forever is the end result. With Jesus, our death is really another birth—a birth into heaven and life with God forever.

As you hang the seed packet ornament, remember the life it contains inside. Remember also that Jesus is the water, the warmth, and the light to the seed of faith God's Holy Spirit planted in us.

Grapevine

"I am the true vine, and My Father is the gardener. He cuts off every branch in Me that bears no fruit, while every branch that does bear fruit He prunes so that it will be even more fruitful. You are already clean because of the work I have spoken to you. Remain in Me and I will remain in you. No branch can bear fruit by itself; it must remain in the vine. Neither can you bear fruit unless you remain in Me. I am the vine; you are the branches. If a man remains in Me and I in him, he will bear much fruit; apart from Me you can do nothing. If anyone does not remain in Me, he is like a branch that is thrown away and withers; such branches are picked up, thrown into the fire and burned. If you remain in Me and My words remain in you, ask whatever you wish, and it will be given you. ...I have told you this so that My joy may be in you and that your joy may be complete."
—JOHN 15:1–7, 11

When a grape falls from the vine, it dies. It lies on the ground in the hot sun, it shrivels, and it dies. Without the vine, the grape has no connection to food or water and it dies. It cannot survive without the protection, nourishment, and connection to life the vine provides.

Jesus said He is the vine and we are the branches full of grapes. If we aren't connected to Jesus, His promises and His love, we are like grapes that have fallen off the vine and we die. If we aren't nourished by His Word, if we don't learn about Him as we grow, we will die. If we aren't protected by His promises, if we aren't nested in His love, we will die.

Jesus connects us to life in God our Father. The only way to the Father is through His Son, Jesus Christ. When we learn about Him, we are nourished by that knowledge. God's Holy Spirit helps us believe in His Word and His promises.

As you hang the vine ornament from your tree, remember the life the vine brings to the grapes and the life Jesus continues to bring to us.

Egg

After the Sabbath, at dawn on the first day of the week, Mary Magdalene and the other Mary went to look at the tomb. There was a violent earthquake, for an angel of the Lord came down from heaven and, going to the tomb, rolled back the stone and sat on it. His appearance was like lightning, and his clothes were white as snow. The guards were so afraid of him that they shook and became like dead men. The angel said to the women, "Do not be afraid, for I know that you are looking for Jesus, who was crucified. He is not here, He has risen, just as He said. Come and see the place where He lay. Then go quickly and tell His disciples: 'He has risen from the dead and is going ahead of you into Galilee. There you will see Him.' Now I have told you." So the women hurried away from the tomb, afraid yet filled with joy, and ran to tell His disciples. Suddenly Jesus met them. "Greetings," He said. They came to Him, clasped His feet and worshiped Him. Then Jesus said to them, "Do not be afraid. Go and tell My brothers to go to Galilee; there they will see Me."

—Matthew 28:1–10

An egg in a chicken coop looks dead. It's hard. It doesn't move. It doesn't appear to grow or change color. It doesn't really seem to do anything. Yet that silly mother hen keeps sitting on that egg. For 21 days, 3 weeks, 504 hours, she protects the egg. She warms it, she moves it, she sits there. At the end of all that time, something amazing happens. A tiny crack appears on the egg. It gets bigger and bigger, until a tiny beak appears. Eventually a chick will come out of the egg—a fuzzy, fluffy ball of life from an egg that appeared to be dead.

When Jesus was killed on the cross, His friends put His body in a tomb. Everyone thought that tomb contained death. But three days later, that tomb was broken open, the stone was rolled away and Life emerged. Jesus had risen! Even death couldn't take Jesus from us—He rose again! Jesus said, "I am the Resurrection." Because we believe in His death and resurrection, we have Jesus' promise that the tomb won't contain us either.

Remember, as you hang the egg ornament on your Advent tree, that we will die one day, but like the chick that comes from the egg and like Jesus leaving the tomb, even though we appear dead, God has promised us life forever!

Peace

---

*"Peace I leave with you; My peace I give you. I
do not give to you as the world gives. Do not let
your hearts be troubled and do not be afraid."*
—JOHN 14:27

The symbol you hang on your tree today is one associated with America in
the 1960s. This was a time in American history of great upset and fear. Two
powerful countries, the United States and the Soviet Union, weren't getting
along very well. Fighting had just ended in Korea and was going on in Vietnam and
several other places. Countries had developed huge weapons that could kill millions

of people instantly. Leaders of some countries were threatening to use the weapons on innocent people. People were upset. People were afraid. People wanted peace and this was the symbol that some people used to represent it.

Peace on earth is hard to come by. Peace among nations today seems impossible in parts of our world. Even peace within nations seems impossible. Sometimes, even families find it difficult to have peace. There is a Latin phrase, "Dona Nobis Pacem" that is also the text of a beautiful song. Translated it means "Grant unto us peace." Read the John 14 passage again. Jesus promises us His peace.

Although people continue to fight and nations continue to battle, in our hearts we can have the peace that passes all human understanding, the peace of God, the peace of knowing we are always loved, the peace of the promise of life eternal—remember this promise as you hang the earthly symbol of peace on your tree.

Noisemakers

"But while he was still a long way off, his father saw him and was filled with compassion for him; he ran to his son, threw his arms around him and kissed him. '...For this son of mine was dead and is alive again; he was lost and is found.' So they began to celebrate."
—LUKE 15: 20, 24

One of the parables Jesus told was about a son. This son asked his father for his inheritance—the money he was to be given when his father died. It was a lot of money, more than he needed to take care of him for the rest of his life. When the money was given to him, he left home at once and was gone for a long, long time. He spent his inheritance foolishly and wastefully and one day, it was all gone. The son had no home, no money, and was ashamed to go back home to tell his father what he had done. He finally decided he had no choice but to return home and hope that his father might give him a job and treat him just like the hired help so he would at least have a warm place to sleep and food to eat. When the son returned home, however, he did not receive the welcome he had expected. While he was still far off, his father saw him coming. His father ran as fast as he could to meet his son. He greeted him with hugs and kisses. He was so thankful his son had returned home that he threw a huge party and invited his friends, his family, and his neighbors to celebrate with him the return of his son. He wasn't angry, he didn't yell—he welcomed his son home again with open arms. The son received so much more than he expected—perhaps even more than he really deserved—not because of what he did, but because of how much his father loved him.

Because of Jesus, God will always do the same for us. No matter how silly we are or what huge mistakes we might make, God will always welcome us home to Him with open arms. Our place in His kingdom, His family, is ours forever. He will always run to greet us. He wants us, He waits for us, He loves us.

As you hang the noisemaker ornament, remember the happy celebration of the return of the son. Remember that, through our baptisms, we were claimed as children of God forever. We are always welcome in His home, we are always loved in His heart. Our return home will be an even bigger and more joyous celebration than the father's son received!

Gift

He sent them to Bethlehem and said, "Go and make a careful search for the child. As soon as you find Him, report to me, so that I too may go and worship Him." After they had heard the king, they went on their way, and the star they had seen in the east went ahead of them until it stopped over the place where the child was. When they saw the star, they were overjoyed. On coming to the house, they saw the child with His mother Mary, and they bowed down and worshiped Him. Then they opened their treasures and presented Him with gifts of gold and of incense and of myrrh.

—MATTHEW 2:8–11

*I*t's probably been several days now since you opened your Christmas gifts. The radio doesn't play Christmas carols anymore. You might be tired of the Christmas decorations, and lots of people have already packed them away until next year. You're back in school now and it hardly even seems like Christmas anymore but it is! Today is the twelfth day of Christmas. Tomorrow we will celebrate the Feast of the Epiphany—the day the wise men brought their gifts to Jesus. One brought gold—riches for someone born to be a king. One brought frankincense which was often burned in a holy place to worship God. One brought myrrh, a spice for burying someone who has died. Jesus was all of the things the gifts represented. He was a King, He was to be worshiped, and He was to die for each of us. These special gifts the wise men carried were brought to Jesus to worship and honor Him.

When you hang your ornament today, remember the gifts of the wise men and think about what gift you could give to Jesus if you were to visit Him today.

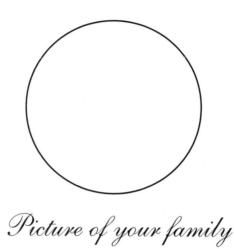

Picture of your family

*So whether you eat or drink or whatever you
do, do it all for the glory of God.*
—1 CORINTHIANS 10:31

Christmas is over. The wise men have delivered their gifts to our King. The time for celebration is past and the time for everyday work and living has arrived. As you hang this final ornament on your Advent tree, you should be reminded of the greatest gift you have to give to God and all of His creation— yourself, your time, and your talents. In thanks and celebration for all the gifts God has given to us, we can give to others. Sometimes we can give smiles and friendship. Sometimes we can do jobs and help with chores. Sometimes we can read stories and write letters.

We don't need to do anything. We can't earn God's love or eternal life—and we don't need to. It has been given to us by the grace of God. Because of that gift and the love we feel for God, however, we share that love with other people. We share our selves, our time, and our talents, knowing that whatever we do in love and service to other people, we do for God.

As you hang this picture of your family on your tree, remember the gifts which you have been given and the gifts you have that you can share with others to spread God's love.

Advent Tree and Ornaments

There are several ways to "make" your Advent tree.

1. Purchase a small, potted evergreen tree. Use it for the Advent and Christmas seasons and plant it outdoors in the spring.
2. Find the branch of an evergreen or other tree and secure it to a sturdy base; hang the ornaments on it.
3. Build your own reusable tree from dowels of various sizes and a supportive base.

Use your imagination with the tree *and* the ornaments. Here are some ideas for ornaments:

1. Photocopy or trace the ornament patterns and have young children color them.
2. Gather the actual items referred to in the text. Tie string to them (or use a glue gun for those you cannot put a hole in) and hang them on the tree.
3. Purchase "shrinky-dink" paper at a sewing or craft store, draw the ornaments, and bake them according to package instructions. (Don't forget to put a hole for the string in the ornament before you bake it!)
4. Cut our circles of construction paper and glue the ornaments to them. Put clear contact paper over the construction paper to protect your work.

The important thing is to enjoy the time you spend on each devotion and making each ornament as a family. Be creative and grow together in Christ.

I am the
Truth

FLOWER
SEEDS